Committee for Environmental Protection (CEP)

I0102481

Non-Native Species Manual

Edition 2016

Secretariat of the Antarctic Treaty
Secrétariat du Traité sur L'Antarctique
Секретариат Договора об Антарктике
Secretaría del Tratado Antártico

Committee for Environmental Protection (CEP)

Non-Native Species Manual

Edition 2016

Secretariat of the Antarctic Treaty

Buenos Aires

2016

Committee for Environmental Protection (CEP)

Non-native Species Manual. Edition 2016.

Buenos Aires: Secretariat of the Antarctic Treaty, 2016.

41 p.

ISBN 978-987-4024-30-5

1. Environmental Protection. 2. International Law. 3. Antarctic Treaty system.

DDC 578.6/2

The first edition of this manual was adopted by the Antarctic Treaty Consultative Meeting through Resolution 6 (2011). The manual was compiled and prepared by an Intersessional Contact Group (ICG) of the Committee for Environmental Protection (CEP) between 2009 and 2011. The second edition of the manual was developed by an ICG of the CEP between 2015 and 2016.

Published by:

Secretariat of the Antarctic Treaty
Secrétariat du Traité sur L'Antarctique
Секретариат Договора об Антарктике
Secretaría del Tratado Antártico

Maipú 757, piso 4
C1006ACI - Ciudad Autónoma
Buenos Aires - Argentina
Tel: +54 11 4320-4250
Fax: +54 11 4320-4253

This book is also available from www.ats.aq (digital version) and online retailers.

ISBN 978-987-4024-30-5

Content

1. Introduction

a) Objective

The overall objective for Parties' actions to address risks posed by non-native species is:

To protect Antarctic biodiversity and intrinsic values by preventing the unintended introduction to the Antarctic region of species not native to that region, and the movement of species within Antarctica from one biogeographic zone to any other.

Preventing unintended introductions is an ambitious goal, consistent with the principles of the Protocol on Environmental Protection to the Antarctic Treaty (1991). In practice, measures should be put in place to minimise the risk of impacts from non-native species in the Antarctic, taking all possible steps towards prevention.

b) Purpose and background

The purpose of this manual is to provide guidance to Antarctic Treaty Parties in order to meet the objective (above), i.e. minimise the risk of accidental or unintentional introduction of non-native species and respond effectively, should an introduction occur. This manual includes key guiding principles and links to recommended practical guidelines and resources that operators can apply and use, as appropriate, to assist with meeting their responsibilities under Annex II to the Protocol. The guidelines are recommendatory, not all guidelines will apply to all operations, and it is a 'living' document that will be updated and added to as new work, research and best practice develops to support further guidance. These measures are recommended as appropriate to assist Parties' efforts to prevent such accidental or unintended introductions or manage established non-native species and they should not be considered as mandatory.

This manual is focused on the unintended or accidental introduction of non-native species. The introduction of non-native species under permit (in accordance with Article 4 of Annex II to the Protocol) is not included within the scope of this work. However, guidelines for response to unintentional introductions can be applied to responding to any dispersal of species intentionally introduced under permits.

Due to a substantial amount of scientific research on non-native species within Antarctica in recent years (see References and supporting information) there is an improved understanding of the risks related to non-native species introductions although additional information will be of benefit. Further studies on impacts on Antarctic ecosystems, and research to underpin effective rapid response are also needed. Another objective of this manual is to support and encourage further work to fill the gaps in our knowledge. Parties, in applying their environmental assessment and authorisation processes, should consider methods to ensure proponents of Antarctic activities are aware of this manual and associated resources, and that they implement prevention practices to minimise the risk of introduction of non-native species.

c) Context[1]

Biological invasions are amongst the most significant threats to biodiversity worldwide, threatening species survival and being responsible for major changes to ecosystem structure and functioning. Despite Antarctica's isolation and harsh climatic conditions, invasions are now recognised as a serious risk to the region: the ice-free areas of Antarctica and the surrounding sub-Antarctic Islands support a large proportion of the world's seabird species, and their terrestrial biotas, though species-poor, include a high proportion of endemic and well-adapted taxa. Species richness in the Southern Ocean is higher than in the Antarctic terrestrial environment, and there is a high level of endemism. With rapid climate change occurring in some parts of Antarctica, increased numbers of introductions and enhanced success of colonisation by non-native species are likely, with consequent increases in impacts on ecosystems, as is already visible in the sub-Antarctic islands. In addition to introduction of species from outside Antarctica, cross-contamination between ice-free areas including isolated nunataks, or between different marine areas, also threatens the biological and genetic diversity of the biogeographic regions and the risk must be addressed. Further development of human activity in these regions (including science, logistics, tourism, fisheries and recreation) will increase the risk of unintentional introductions of organisms, which have a suite of life history traits that benefit them during transport, establishment and expansion phases of invasion, and are likely to be favored by warming conditions and potentially other effects of climate

---

[1] This section was written with the contribution of several scientists involved in the IPY "Aliens in Antarctica" project (D. Bergstrom, S. Chown, P. Convey, Y. Frenot, N. Gremmen, A. Huiskes, K. A. Hughes, S. Imura, M. Lebouvier, J. Lee, F. Steenhuisen, M.Tsujimoto, B. van de Vijver and J. Whinam) and adapted according to the ICG Members' comments.

change. Reducing the risk of the transfer of species between sites in Antarctica has been a recent focus of work to manage non-native species risks. In 2012 CEP XV endorsed 15 distinct Antarctic Conservation Biogeographic Regions. The delineation of these biologically distinct regions supports the management of non-native species risks associated with moving between regions within Antarctica.

The vast majority of global non-native species do not become invasive, but those that do are one of the main threats to global diversity. Sequentially, the prevention of an introduction of a non-native species is the key. If prevention fails, then early detection and rapid response to remove the species becomes very important. It is easier to fight invasiveness if the discovery of the non-native species is made early. In addition, the presence of non-native species that are only "transient" or "persistent" but not yet "invasive" is also highly undesirable in terms of protecting the environmental and scientific values of Antarctica, especially as such species may become invasive. The current environmental changes that occur in Antarctica, as in other parts of the world, may result in alteration of the local biodiversity during the next decades or centuries. It is the responsibility of the Parties and others active in the region to minimise the chance of humans being a direct vector for change through introduction of non-native species and/or spread of diseases in the terrestrial and marine ecosystems of the Antarctic Treaty area.

The 2010 Antarctic Treaty Meeting of Experts on Implications of Climate Change for Antarctic Management emphasised the importance of actions towards reducing the risk and impact of non-native species to Antarctic ecosystems. The meeting:

•   Acknowledged that the greatest effort should be placed on preventing the introduction of non-native species, and on minimising the risk of human assisted introductions through national programmes and tourism activities. It stressed the importance of ensuring comprehensive implementation of new measures to address this risk (Para. 111, Co-chair's report).

•   Recommended that the CEP 'consider using established methods of identifying a) Antarctic environments at high risk from establishment by non-natives and b) non-native species that present a high risk of establishment in Antarctica' (Recommendation 22).

•   Recommended that Parties be encouraged to comprehensively and consistently implement management measures to respond to the environmental implications of climate change, particularly measures to avoid introduction and translocation of non-native species, and to report on their effectiveness (Recommendation 23).

In 2015, the CEP agreed the Climate Change Response Work Programme (CCRWP) that seeks to advance these and other environment-related ATME recommendations (Resolution 4 (2015)). The CCRWP describes the issues facing the CEP as a result of the changing Antarctic climate, the actions/tasks required to address these issues, their prioritisation, and suggestions as to how, when, and by whom, the actions are best delivered. One of the climate-related issues identified is the enhanced potential for non-native species introduction and establishment. The CCRWP recommends that CEP Members continue to develop the CEP Non-native Species Manual, ensuring climate change impacts are included, specifically in the development of surveillance approaches, a response strategy, and the inclusion of non-native species in the EIA guidelines (see also the Annex to this manual).

The CEP 5-year Work Plan is a 'living' document that is updated annually with the work priorities of the Committee. Non-native species issues are identified in the work plan as a top priority for the CEP's attention and the work plan and may guide further work on this topic.

The Environments Portal (www.environments.aq) is a source of peer-reviewed Antarctic environmental information and includes topic summaries on non-native species (e.g. Newman et al., 2014; Hughes and Frenot, 2015).

d) Glossary

Terminology for non-native and invasive species has not been standardised internationally and some of the terms below are defined in the specific context of Antarctica:

Biogeographic region: a region of Antarctica that is biologically distinct from other regions. Non-native species risks to biodiversity and intrinsic values may arise if (1) native Antarctic species are moved by human activities between biogeographic regions, or (2) non-native species established in one Antarctic biogeographic region are distributed to other regions by human or natural mechanisms.

Containment: Application of management measures to prevent spread of a non-native species.

Control: Use of practical methods to contain and/or reduce the viability of a non-native species.

Endemic: native species restricted to a specified region or locality in Antarctica.

Eradication: The permanent elimination of a non-native species.

Introduction/introduced: direct or indirect movement by human agency, of an organism outside its natural range. This term may be applied to intercontinental or intracontinental movement of species.

Invasive/invasion: non-native species that are extending their range in the colonised Antarctic region, displacing native species and causing significant harm to biological diversity or ecosystem functioning.

Non-native/alien species: an organism occurring outside its natural past or present range and dispersal potential, whose presence and dispersal in any biogeographic region of the Antarctic Treaty area is due to unintentional human action.

Persistent/established: non-native species that have survived, established and reproduced for many years in a restricted locality in Antarctica, but which have not expanded their range from a specific location.

Transient: non-native species that have survived in small populations for a short period in Antarctica, but which have either died out naturally or have been removed by human intervention.

2. Key guiding principles

In order to provide greater focus on the environmental risk related to the unintentional introduction of non-native species in Antarctica and to guide Parties' actions in accordance with the overall objective, 11 key guiding principles have been developed. They are categorised according to the three major components of a non-native species management framework: prevention, monitoring and response. Many of the key guiding principles are equally applicable to the prevention of introduction and spread of pathogens that may cause diseases in Antarctic wildlife.

Prevention

Prevention is the most effective means of minimising the risks associated with the introduction of non-native species and their impacts, and is the responsibility of all who travel to Antarctica.

1. Raising awareness at multiple levels for different audiences is a critical component of management. All people travelling to the Antarctic should take appropriate steps to prevent the introduction of non-native species.

2. The risk of non-native species introductions should be identified and addressed in the planning of all activities, including through the environmental impact assessment (EIA) process under Article 8 and Annex I to the Protocol.

3. In the absence of sound scientific baseline data, a precautionary approach should be applied to minimise the risk of human-mediated introduction of non-native species, as well as the risk of inter-regional and local transfer of propagules to pristine regions.

4. Preventive measures are most likely to be implemented and effective if they are:

- focused on addressing activities and areas of highest risk;

- developed to suit the particular circumstances of the activity or area in question, and at the appropriate scale;

- technically and logistically simple;

- easily applicable;

- cost effective and not exceedingly time consuming.

5. Prevention should focus on pre-departure measures within the logistics and supply chain:

- at the point of origin outside Antarctica (e.g., cargo, personal gear, packages),

- at gateways to Antarctica (ports, airports),

- on means of transport (vessels, aircraft),

- at Antarctic stations and field camps that are departure points for activities within the continent.

6. Particularly close attention should be given to ensuring the cleanliness of items previously used in cold climates (e.g., Arctic, sub-Antarctic, mountainous areas), which may be a means for transporting species with 'pre-adaptations' that may aid establishment in the Antarctic environment.

Monitoring

Monitoring can be passive observation (i.e., waiting for non-native species to appear) or targeted (i.e., an active programme of identifying potential non-native species). Having good baseline data on native fauna and flora is important to support monitoring of non-native species.

7. Regular/periodic monitoring, with a frequency appropriate to potential risk, of high-risk sites (e.g., including, but not restricted to the area around research stations) should be encouraged.

8. Preventive measures should be periodically reviewed and revised.

9. Information and best practice related to non-native species should be exchanged between Parties and other stakeholders.

Response

The key factor will be to respond quickly and to assess the feasibility and desirability of eradicating non-native species. If eradication is not a feasible or desirable option then control and/or containment measures need to be considered.

10. To be effective, responses to introductions should be undertaken as a priority, to prevent an increase in the species' distribution range and to make eradication simpler, cost effective and more likely to succeed.

11. Efficacy of control or eradication programmes must be regularly assessed, including follow-up surveys.

3. Guidelines and resources to support prevention of the introduction of non-native species

including the transfer of species between sites in the Antarctic and the detection of and response to established non-native species. In line with the objective for Parties' actions to address risks posed by non-native species and the key guiding principles (Sections 1 and 2), the following voluntary guidelines and resources have been developed that operators can apply and use, as appropriate, to assist with meeting their responsibilities under Annex II to the Protocol.

Prevention

1. The environmental impact assessment process is a key component in the prevention of non-native species introductions and their further dispersal.

Guidelines

Guidelines for Environmental Impact Assessment in Antarctica

http://www.ats.aq/documents/ATCM39/att/atcm39_att013_rev1_e.doc

2. Prevention is the most effective means of minimizing the risks associated with the introduction of non-native species.

Guidelines:

The following list provides general guidance on preventing non-native species introductions to Antarctica, with more specific information detailed later:

• Unless new, ensure clothing supplied for use in Antarctica is cleaned using normal laundry procedures prior to sending to Antarctica. Pre-worn footwear should be cleaned thoroughly before arrival in Antarctica or between sites in Antarctica.

• Consider equipping research stations with the means to clean and maintain clothing and equipment that is to be used in the field, particularly in distinct or multiple locations.

• Check cargo to ensure it is clean of visible contamination (soil, mud, vegetation, propagules) before loading on board the aircraft or vessels.

• Clean vehicles in order to prevent transfer of non-native species into and around the Antarctic.

- Confirm vessels as being rodent-free before departure to the Antarctic.

- Pack, store and load cargo in an area with a clean, sealed surface (e.g., bitumen or concrete that is free from weedy plants, soil, rodents and remote from waste ground). These areas should be cleaned and inspected regularly.

- Containers, including ISO containers and boxes/crates, should not be moved from one Antarctic site to another, unless they are cleaned before arrival at the new location.

- Ensure intercontinental aircraft are checked and treated as necessary, where applicable, to ensure they are insect-free before departure to the Antarctic.

- Foods and food wastes are strictly managed to prevent them entering the environment (e.g. secured from wildlife and removed from the Antarctic or incinerated).

At CEP XV, the Committee recognised the relevance of the Antarctic Conservation Biogeographic Regions (ACBRs) to its work to address non-native species risks, particularly the risk of transfer of species between biologically distinct locations in Antarctica. Descriptions of the Antarctic Conservation Biogeographic Regions can be found at: http://www.ats.aq/documents/recatt/Att500_e.pdf. The Antarctic Environments Portal Map shows in detail the extent of the Antarctic Conservation Biogeographic Regions and is available from: https://environments.aq/map/

Procedures for vehicle cleaning to prevent transfer of non-native species into and around Antarctica (ATCM XXXIII – WP 08).

http://www.ats.aq/documents/ATCM33/wp/ATCM33_wp008_e.doc

Guidelines to minimise the risks of non-native species and disease associated with Antarctic hydroponics facilities (ATCM XXXV – WP 25 rev.1)

http://www.ats.aq/documents/ATCM35/wp/ATCM35_wp025_rev1_e.doc

http://www.ats.aq/documents/ATCM35/att/ATCM35_att103_e.doc

Resources:

Checklists for supply chain managers of National Antarctic Programmes for the reduction in risk of transfer of non-native species (COMNAP, SCAR 2010)
https://www.comnap.aq/Shared%20Documents/nnschecklists.pdf

SCAR's environmental code of conduct for terrestrial scientific field research in Antarctica (ATCM XXXII - IP 04)

http://www.ats.aq/documents/ATCM32/ip/ATCM32_ip004_e.doc

SCAR's code of conduct for activities within terrestrial geothermal environments in Antarctica Resolution 3 (2016)

http://www.ats.aq/documents/ATCM39/att/atcm39_att018_e.doc

SCAR's code of conduct for the exploration and research of subglacial aquatic environments (ATCM XXXIV- IP 33)

http://www.ats.aq/documents/ATCM34/ip/ATCM34_ip033_e.doc

Raising awareness of non-native species introductions: Workshop results and checklists for supply chain managers (ATCM XXXIV – WP 12)

http://www.ats.aq/documents/ATCM34/wp/ATCM34_wp012_e.doc

http://www.ats.aq/documents/ATCM34/att/ATCM34_att014_e.pdf

http://www.ats.aq/documents/ATCM34/att/ATCM34_att015_e.pdf

Reducing the risk of inadvertent non-native species introductions associated with fresh fruit and vegetable importation to Antarctica (ATCM XXXV – WP 06)

http://www.ats.aq/documents/ATCM35/wp/ATCM35_WP006_e.doc

Biosecurity and quarantine guidelines for ACAP breeding sites

http://acap.aq/en/resources/acap-conservation-guidelines/2180-biosecurity-guidelines/file

Outcomes of the International Polar Year Programme: Aliens in Antarctica (ATCM XXXV – WP 05)

http://www.ats.aq/documents/ATCM35/wp/ATCM35_wp005_e.doc

Continent-wide risk assessment for the establishment of nonindigenous species in Antarctica (ATCM XXXV – BP 01)

http://www.ats.aq/documents/ATCM35/bp/ATCM35_bp001_e.pdf

3. Develop and deliver awareness programmes for all people travelling to and working in the Antarctic on the risks of inter and intra-continental movements of non-native species and on the measures required to prevent their introduction,

16

including a standard set of key messages for awareness programmes. Education and training programmes should be tailored, in some case using relevant elements of the information listed above, to the activities and risks associated with the target audience, including:

- Managers of national programmes

- Logisticians/crew/contractors

- Tour operators/staff/crew

- Scientists

- Tourists

- Private expedition organisers

- Fishing vessel operators/staff/crew

- Staff at suppliers/vendors/warehouses

- Other visitors

Guidelines:

General guidelines for visitors to the Antarctic

http://www.ats.aq/documents/recatt/Att483_e.pdf

Resources:

Instructional video on cleaning (Aliens in Antarctica Project, 2010).

http://academic.sun.ac.za/cib/video/Aliens_cleaning_video%202010.wmv

'Don't pack a pest' pamphlet (United States).

http://www.usap.gov/usapgov/travelAndDeployment/documents/PackaPest_brochure_Final.pdf

'Don't pack a pest' pamphlet (IAATO).

http://iaato.org/en_GB/dont-pack-a-pest

Boot, clothing and equipment decontamination guidelines (IAATO).

http://iaato.org/documents/10157/14310/Boot_Washing07.pdf/2527fa99-b3b9-4848-bf0b-b1b595ecd046

'Know before you go' pamphlet (ASOC).

http://www.asoc.org/storage/documents/tourism/ASOC_Know_Before_You_Go_tourist_pamphlet_2009_editionv2.pdf

COMNAP Practical training modules: Module 2 – non-native species (ATCMXXXVIII – IP 101)

http://www.ats.aq/documents/ATCM38/ip/ATCM38_ip101_e.doc

http://www.ats.aq/documents/ATCM38/att/ATCM38_att102_e.pdf

4. Include consideration of non-native species in future ASPA and ASMA Management Plans and in the review of current and future management plans.

Guidelines:

Guide to the preparation of Management Plans for Antarctic Specially Protected Areas (Resolution 2 (2011)).

http://www.ats.aq/documents/ATCM34/att/ATCM34_att004_e.doc

5. Manage ballast water in accordance with the 'Practical guidelines for ballast water exchange in the Antarctic Treaty Area' (Resolution 3 (2006)).

Guidelines:

Practical guidelines for ballast water exchange in the Antarctic Treaty Area (Resolution 3 (2006)).

http://www.ats.aq/documents/recatt/Att345_e.pdf

Monitoring

6. Record non-native species introductions and submit records to the 'Biodiversity database: aliens species in the Antarctica or subAntarctic', managed by the Australian Antarctic Data Centre (AADC), as agreed by the CEP.

Database for entering records:

Alien species database (ATCM XXXIV – IP 68)

http://data.aad.gov.au/aadc/biodiversity/index_aliens.cfm

Resources:

Colonisation status of known non-native species in the Antarctic terrestrial environment: a review. (ATCM XXXVIII IP 46)

http://www.ats.aq/documents/ATCM38/ip/ATCM38_IP046_e.doc

Biological invasions in terrestrial Antarctica: what is the current status and how can we respond? (ATCM XXXVIII - IP 46 Attachment A)

http://www.ats.aq/documents/ATCM38/att/ATCM38_att090_e.pdf

Supplementary information (ATCM XXXVIII - IP 46 Attachment B)

http://www.ats.aq/documents/ATCM38/att/ATCM38_att091_e.doc

Monitoring biological invasion across the broader Antarctic: a baseline and indicator framework (ATCM XXXVIII – IP 93)

http://www.ats.aq/documents/ATCM38/ip/ATCM38_IP093_e.doc

Status of known non-native species introductions and impacts (Environments Portal)

https://www.environments.aq/information-summaries/status-of-known-non-native-species-introductions-and-impacts/

Response

A species apparently new to the Antarctic may be (i) a recent natural colonist (e.g. introduced by wind or bird transport), (ii) a recent human introduction (e.g. associated with cargo, clothing or personal belongings) or (iii) a long-term inhabitant that has never before been identified by science. It is important to know the colonisation history of a new species as this will affect how it is managed.

7. Develop or employ assessment metrics to help determine whether a newly discovered species is likely to have arrived through natural colonisation pathways or through human means.

8. Expert advice should be sought as quickly as possible when potential non-native species (including any diseases of wildlife) are detected.

Guidelines:

Guidance for visitors and environmental managers following the discovery of a suspected non-native species in the terrestrial and freshwater Antarctic environment (ATCM XXXIII - WP 15).

http://www.ats.aq/documents/ATCM33/att/ATCM33_att010_e.doc

http://www.ats.aq/documents/ATCM33/att/ATCM33_att011_e.doc

Resource:

SCAR is well placed to assist with the identification of experts that could provide appropriate advice in a timely manner. SCAR has agreed to identify a group of experts who could be consulted in the event that a suspected non-native species is detected. If a non-native species is detected, contact with the group could be facilitated through the Chief Officer of the SCAR Standing Committee on the Antarctic Treaty System (SCATS), who would then co-ordinate and collate the response from the experts.

Suggested framework and considerations for scientists attempting to determine the colonisation status of newly discovered terrestrial or freshwater species within the Antarctic Treaty Area (ATCM XXXIII – IP 44).

http://www.ats.aq/documents/ATCM33/ip/ATCM33_ip044_e.doc

Annex: Guidelines and resources requiring further attention or development

In addition to the measures, guidelines and resources that have been developed (Section 3) the following non-native species issues have been identified as requiring further attention and policy development. The use of existing guidelines, resources and information and the development of more detailed guidance under these items for inclusion in the Manual are encouraged.

Prevention

No.	Guidelines and resources requiring further attention or development	Existing guidelines, resources or information
1	Reducing the distribution of native Antarctic species between distinct biogeographic regions within the continent: • Identify regions of highest risk of introduction. • Identify activities, vectors and pathways that present a high risk to different biogeographical regions • Provide guidance on what constitutes a gateway between Antarctic biogeographical regions (according to organism type). • Develop practical measures to address risks associated with the transport of personnel and equipment between locations in Antarctica. • Develop baseline studies.	Antarctic Conservation Biogeographic Regions (ACBRs) http://www.ats.aq/documents/recatt/Att500_e.pdf The Antarctic Environments Portal Map shows the extent of the Antarctic Conservation Biogeographic Regions and is available from: https://environments.aq/map/ Current knowledge for reducing risks posed by terrestrial non-native species: towards an evidence-based approach (ATCM XXXIII - WP 06). http://www.ats.aq/documents/ATCM33/wp/ATCM33_wp006_e.doc A framework for analysing and managing non-native species risks in Antarctica (ATCM XXXII - IP 36). http://www.ats.aq/documents/ATCM32/ip/ATCM32_ip036_e.doc ATCM XXXIII - WP 14 (United Kingdom) 2010 - Intra-regional transfer of species in terrestrial Antarctica. http://www.ats.aq/documents/ATCM33/wp/ATCM33_wp014_e.doc

No.	Guidelines and resources requiring further attention or development	Existing guidelines, resources or information
2	Preventing further distribution of existing non-native species to other Antarctica locations: • Provide guidance, and develop practical biosecurity measures, to reduce anthropogenic transfer of non-native species within Antarctica. • Provide guidance on reducing natural transfer of non-native species within Antarctica.	Colonisation status of known non-native species in the Antarctic terrestrial environment: a review. Attachment A: Biological invasions in terrestrial Antarctica: what is the current status and how can we respond? Attachment B: Supplementary information (ATCM XXXVIII – IP 46) http://www.ats.aq/documents/ATCM38/ip/ATCM38_IP046_e.doc http://www.ats.aq/documents/ATCM38/att/ATCM38_att090_e.pdf http://www.ats.aq/documents/ATCM38/att/ATCM38_att091_e.doc
3	Identifying potential non-native species that present a high risk to Antarctic environments: • Generate a list, with suitable descriptions, of potential non-native species based on the experience of the sub-Antarctic Islands (or other relevant environments) and the biological characteristics and adaptability of the "effective" colonisers.	Current knowledge for reducing risks posed by terrestrial non-native species: towards an evidence-based approach. Appendix 1 – Risk assessment protocol for springtails developed by Greenslade (2002: page 341) (ATCM XXXIII - WP 06) http://www.ats.aq/documents/ATCM33/wp/ATCM33_wp6_e.doc http://www.ats.aq/documents/ATCM33/att/ATCM33_att005_e.doc

No.	Guidelines and resources requiring further attention or development	Existing guidelines, resources or information
4	Preventing non-native species introductions to the Antarctic marine environment: • Improve understanding of risks and pathways for introduction. • Undertake a risk assessment to identify marine habitats at risk of invasion. • Develop specific guidelines.	
5	Addressing non-native species (including microorganisms) risk associated with wastewater discharge, including disease risk to local wildlife (see later section on Diseases): • Improve understanding of risks and pathways for introduction. • Develop specific guidelines to reduce non-native species release with wastewater discharge.	New records of the presence of human associated microorganisms in the Antarctic marine environment (ATCM XXXV – WP 55) http://www.ats.aq/documents/ATCM35/wp/ATCM35_wp055_e.doc Discharge of sewage and grey water from vessels in Antarctic Treaty waters (ATCM XXXVI – IP 66) http://www.ats.aq/documents/ATCM36/ip/ATCM36_ip066_e.doc Assessment of environmental impacts arising from sewage discharge at Davis Station (ATCM XXXV – BP10) http://www.ats.aq/documents/ATCM35/bp/ATCM35_bp010_e.doc Reducing sewage pollution in the Antarctic marine environment using a sewage treatment plant (ATCM XXVIII – IP37) http://www.ats.aq/documents/ATCM28/ip/ATCM28_ip037_e.doc Wastewater treatment in Antarctica: challenges and process improvements (ATCM XXIX – IP60)

No.	Guidelines and resources requiring further attention or development	Existing guidelines, resources or information
		http://www.ats.aq/documents/ATCM29/ip/ATCM29_ip060_e.doc
6	Limiting introductions or redistribution of microorganisms that might impact upon existing microbial communities in the Antarctic environment: • Improve understanding of risks and pathways for introductions. • Develop more specific guidelines for preventing introductions and/or redistribution of microorganisms in the Antarctic environment.	Human footprint in Antarctica and the long-term conservation of terrestrial microbial habitats (ATCM XXXVI - WP 39) http://www.ats.aq/documents/ATCM36/wp/ATCM36_wp039_e.doc SCAR's code of conduct for the exploration and research of subglacial aquatic environments (ATCM XXXIV- IP 33) http://www.ats.aq/documents/ATCM34/ip/ATCM34_ip033_e.doc

No.	Guidelines and resources requiring further attention or development	Existing guidelines, resources or information
7	Monitoring for non-native species in the Antarctic marine and terrestrial environments: • Develop generally applicable monitoring guidelines. More detailed or site-specific monitoring may be required for particular locations. • Implement marine and terrestrial monitoring following the development of a monitoring framework. • Identify who will undertake the monitoring and with what frequency. • A status report on established monitoring should be submitted regularly to the CEP.	Summary of environmental monitoring and reporting discussions (ATCM XXXI – IP 07) http://www.ats.aq/documents/ATCM31/ip/ATCM31_ip007_e.doc

No.	Guidelines and resources requiring further attention or development	Existing guidelines, resources or information
8	Establishing which native species are present at Antarctic sites to assist with identifying scale and scope of current and future introductions (because it is not practical to conduct surveys everywhere, priority should be given to sites of high human activity (i.e. stations, most frequently visited scientific field sites and visitor sites), high value and/or high sensitivity): • Compile existing biodiversity data (including from terrestrial, aquatic and marine ecosystems). • Develop guidelines on undertaking baseline biodiversity surveys.	Final report on the research project 'The impact of human activities on soil organisms of the maritime Antarctic and the introduction of non-native species in Antarctica' (ATCM XXXVI – IP 55) http://www.ats.aq/documents/ATCM36/ip/ATCM36_ip055_e.doc http://www.umweltbundesamt.de/uba-info-medien/4416.html

Response

No.	Guidelines and resources requiring further attention or development	Existing guidelines, resources or information
9	Responding rapidly to non-native species introductions: • Develop guidelines on rapid response, including information on practical eradication or containment/control of plants, invertebrates and other biological groups.	Eradication of a vascular plant species recently introduced to Whalers Bay, Deception Island (United Kingdom, Spain 2010) http://www.ats.aq/documents/ATCM33/ip/ATCM33_ip043_e.doc The successful eradication of *Poa pratensis* from Cierva Point, Danco Coast, Antarctic Peninsula (Argentina, Spain and the United Kingdom, 2015) http://www.ats.aq/documents/ATCM38/ip/ATCM38_ip029_e.doc Eradication of a non-native grass *Poa annua* L. from ASPA No 128 Western Shore of Admiralty Bay, King George Island, South Shetland Islands (Poland, 2015) http://www.ats.aq/documents/ATCM38/ip/ATCM38_ip078_e.doc

No.	Guidelines and resources requiring further attention or development	Existing guidelines, resources or information
10	Taking steps to reduce the risk of introducing plant and animal pathogens to Antarctica and their subsequent dispersal within the region by human activity: • Develop (or formally adopt existing) guidance for responding to disease events. • Introduce preventive measures to diminish risks of introduction of diseases to Antarctic wildlife, for example, specific guidance for handling field and station waste to minimise introduction of non-native species. • Develop specific cleaning requirements that may be needed if there is reason to think that people, clothing, equipment or vehicles have been in contact with diseased animals, disease causing agents or have been in an area of known disease risk.	Report on the open-ended intersessional contact group on diseases of Antarctic wildlife. Report 2 – Practical measures to diminish risk (draft) (Australia, 2001) http://www.ats.aq/documents/ATCM24/wp/ATCM24_wp011_e.pdf Study to determine occurrence of non-native species introduced into Antarctica through natural pathways (Argentina, 2015) http://www.ats.aq/documents/ATCM38/wp/ATCM38_wp046_e.doc Health of Antarctic Wildlife: A challenge for science and policy (Kerry and Riddle, 2009). Although unusual animal mortality events may occur for a variety of reasons, disease may be a likely cause. Therefore the following resources may be relevant: Mass animal mortality event response plan (British Antarctic Survey). Available from BAS. https://www.bas.ac.uk/ Unusual mortality response plan (Australia), referred to in: http://www.ats.aq/documents/ATCM27/ip/ATCM27_ip071_e.doc Procedures for reporting a high mortality event (IAATO): Available from IAATO. http://iaato.org/ http://www.ats.aq/documents/ATCM39/ip/ATCM39_ip119_e.doc

References and supporting information

Note: The Environments Portal (www.environments.aq) is a source of peer-reviewed Antarctic environmental information and includes topic summaries on non-native species (e.g. Newman et al., 2014; Hughes and Frenot, 2015).

ATCM XXII - IP 04 (Australia) 1998 - Introduction of diseases to Antarctic wildlife: Proposed workshop.

ATCM XXIII - WP 32 (Australia) 1999 - Report to ATCM XXIII on outcomes from the Workshop on diseases of Antarctic wildlife.

ATCM XXIV - WP 10 (Australia) 2001 - Report on the open-ended intersessional contact group on diseases of Antarctic wildlife: Report 1 - Review and risk assessment.

ATCM XXIV - WP 11 (Australia) 2001 - Report on the open-ended intersessional contact group on diseases of Antarctic wildlife: Report 2 - Practical measures to diminish risk (draft).

ATCM XXV - IP 62 (Australia) 2002 - Draft response plan in the event that unusual animal deaths are discovered.

ATCM XXVII - IP 71 (Australia) 2004 - Australia's Antarctic quarantine practices.

ATCM XXVIII - WP 28 (Australia) 2005 - Measures to address the unintentional introduction and spread of non-native biota and disease to the Antarctic Treaty Area.

ATCM XXVIII - IP37 (United Kingdom) 2005 - Reducing sewage pollution in the Antarctic marine environment using a sewage treatment plant.

ATCM XXVIII - IP 97 (IAATO) 2005 - Update on boot and clothing decontamination guidelines and the introduction and detection of diseases in Antarctic wildlife: IAATO's perspective.

ATCM XXIX - WP 05 Rev. 1 (United Kingdom) 2006 - Practical guidelines for ballast water exchange in the Antarctic Treaty Area.

ATCM XXIX - IP 44 (Australia) 2006 - Principles underpinning Australia's approach to Antarctic quarantine management.

ATCM XXIX - IP60 (United States) 2006 - Wastewater treatment in Antarctica: challenges and process improvements.

ATCM XXX - IP 49 (Australia, SCAR) 2007 - Aliens in Antarctica.

ATCM XXXI - WP 16 (Australia) - Antarctic alien species database.

ATCM XXXI - IP 07 (Australia) 2008 - Summary of environmental monitoring and reporting discussions.

ATCM XXXI - IP 17 (Australia, China, India, Romania, Russian Federation) 2008 - Measures to protect the Larsemann Hills, East Antarctica, from the introduction of non-native species.

ATCM XXXI - IP 98 (COMNAP) - Survey on existing procedures concerning introduction of non native species in Antarctica.

ATCM XXXII - WP 05 (Australia, France, New Zealand) 2009 - A work program for CEP action on non-native species.

ATCM XXXII - WP 23 (South Africa) 2009 - Propagule transport associated with logistic operations: a South African appraisal of a regional issue.

ATCM XXXII - WP 32 (United Kingdom) 2009 - Procedures for vehicle cleaning to prevent transfer of non-native species into and around Antarctica.

ATCM XXXII - WP 33 (United Kingdom) 2009 - Review of provisions relating to non-native species introductions in ASPA and ASMA management plans.

ATCM XXXII - IP 04 (SCAR) 2009 - SCAR's environmental code of conduct for terrestrial scientific field research in Antarctica.

ATCM XXXII - IP 12 (United Kingdom) 2009 - ASPA and ASMA management plans: review of provisions relating to non-native species introductions.

ATCM XXXII - SP 11 (ATS) 2009 - Topic summary of CEP discussions on non-native species (NNS) in Antarctica.

ATCM XXXIII - WP 04 (SCAR) 2010 - Preliminary results from the International Polar Year Programme: Aliens in Antarctica.

ATCM XXXIII - WP 06 (SCAR, Australia) 2010 - Current knowledge for reducing risks posed by terrestrial non-native species: towards an evidence-based approach.

ATCM XXXIII - WP 08 (United Kingdom) 2010 - Draft procedures for vehicle cleaning to prevent transfer of non-native species into and around Antarctica.

ATCM XXXIII - WP 09 (France) 2010 - Open-ended Intersessional Contact Group on "Non-native species" (NNS) - 2009-2010 report.

ATCM XXXIII - WP 14 (United Kingdom) 2010 - Intra-regional transfer of species in terrestrial Antarctica.

ATCM XXXIII - WP 15 (United Kingdom) 2010 - Guidance for visitors and environmental managers following the discovery of a suspected non-native species in the terrestrial and freshwater Antarctic environment.

ATCM XXXIII - IP 43 (United Kingdom, Spain) 2010 - Eradication of a vascular plant species recently introduced to Whaler's Bay, Deception Island.

ATCM XXXIII - IP 44 (United Kingdom) 2010 - Suggested framework and considerations for scientists attempting to determine the colonisation status of newly discovered terrestrial or freshwater species within the Antarctic Treaty Area.

ATCM XXXIV - WP 12 (COMNAP and SCAR) 2011 - Raising awareness of non-native species introductions: Workshop results and checklists for supply chain managers.

ATCM XXXIV - WP 34 (New Zealand) 2011 – Report of the Intersessional Contact Group on non-native species 2010-2011.

ATCM XXXIV - WP 53 (SCAR) 2011 - Measures to reduce the risk of non-native species introductions to the Antarctic region associated with fresh foods.

ATCM XXXIV - IP 26 (Germany) 2011 - Progress report on the research project "The role of human activities in the introduction of non-native species into Antarctica and in the distribution of organisms within the Antarctic".

ATCM XXXIV - IP 32 (France) 2011 – Report on the IPY Oslo Science Conference session on non-native species.

ATCM XXXIV IP 50 (United Kingdom and Uruguay) 2011 – Colonisation status of known non-native species in the Antarctic terrestrial environment (update 2011).

ATCM XXXIV - IP 68 (Australia and SCAR) 2011 - Alien species database.

ATCM XXXV - WP 05 (SCAR) 2012 – Outcomes of the International Polar Year programme: Aliens in Antarctica.

ATCM XXXV - WP 06 (SCAR) 2012 – Reducing the risk of inadvertent non-native species introductions associated with fresh fruit and vegetable importation to Antarctica.

ATCM XXXV - WP 25 rev.1 (Australia and France) 2012 – Guidelines to minimise the risks of non-native species and disease associated with Antarctic hydroponics facilities.

ATCM XXXV - WP 55 (Chile) 2012 – New records of the presence of human associated microorganisms in the Antarctic marine environment.

ATCM XXXV - IP 13 (Spain, Argentina and the United Kingdom) 2012 – Colonisation status of the non-native grass Poa pratensis at Cierva Point, Danco Coast, Antarctic Peninsula.

ATCM XXXV - IP 29 (United Kingdom) 2012 – Colonisation status of known non-native species in the Antarctic terrestrial environment (update 2012).

ATCM XXXV - BP 01 (SCAR) 2012 – Continent-wide risk assessment for the establishment of nonindigenous species in Antarctica.

ATCM XXXV - BP 010 (Australia) 2012 – Assessment of environmental impacts arising from sewage discharge at Davis Station.

ATCM XXXVI - WP 19 (Germany) 2013 - Report on the research project "The impact of human activities on soil organisms of the maritime Antarctic and the introduction of non-native species in Antarctica".

ATCM XXXVI - WP 39 (Belgium, SCAR, South Africa and the United Kingdom) 2013 - Human footprint in Antarctica and the long-term conservation of terrestrial microbial habitats.

ATCM XXXVI - IP 28 (United Kingdom) 2013 – Colonisation status of known non-native species in the Antarctic terrestrial environment (update 2013).

ATCM XXXVI - IP 35 (Argentina, Spain and the United Kingdom) 2013 - The non-native grass Poa pratensis at Cierva Point, Danco Coast, Antarctic Peninsula – on-going investigations and future eradication plans.

ATCM XXXVI - IP 55 (Germany) 2013 - Final report on the research project "The impact of human activities on soil organisms of the maritime Antarctic and the introduction of non-native species in Antarctica".

ATCM XXXVI - IP 66 (ASOC) 2013 - Discharge of sewage and grey water from vessels in Antarctic Treaty waters.

ATCM XXXVII - WP 04 (Germany) 2014 - Report on the informal discussion on tourism and the risk of introducing non-native organisms.

ATCM XXXVII - IP 23 (United Kingdom) 2014 - Colonisation status of known non-native species in the Antarctic terrestrial environment (update 2014).

ATCM XXXVII - IP 83 (Argentina) 2014 - Record of two species of non-native birds at 25 de Mayo Island, South Shetland Islands.

ATCM XXXVIII - WP 37 (Norway and the United Kingdom) 2015 – Report from ICG on climate change.

ATCM XXXVIII - WP 46 (Argentina) 2015 - Study to determine occurrence of non-native species introduced into Antarctica through natural pathways.

ATCM XXXVIII - IP 29 (Argentina, Spain and the United Kingdom) 2015 - The successful eradication of Poa pratensis from Cierva Point, Danco Coast, Antarctic Peninsula.

ATCM XXXVIII - IP 46 (United Kingdom, Chile and Spain) 2015 - Colonisation status of known non-native species in the Antarctic terrestrial environment: a review. Attachment A: Biological invasions in terrestrial Antarctica: what is the current status and how can we respond? Attachment B: Supplementary information.

ATCM XXXVIII - IP 78 (Poland) 2015 - Eradication of a non-native grass Poa annua L. from ASPA No. 128 Western Shore of Admiralty Bay, King George Island, South Shetland Islands.

ATCM XXXVIII - IP 93 (SCAR) Monitoring biological invasion across the broader Antarctic: a baseline and indicator framework.

ATCM XXXVIII - IP 101 (COMNAP) 2015 - COMNAP practical training modules: Module 2 - Non-native species.

Augustyniuk-Kram, A., Chwedorzewska, K.J., Korczak-Abshire, M., Olech, M., Lityńska–Zając, M. 2013 - An analysis of fungal propagules transported to the Henryk Arctowski Station. Pol. Polar Res. 34, 269–278.

Chown, S.L., Convey, P. 2007 - Spatial and temporal variability across life's hierarchies in the terrestrial Antarctic. Phil. Trans. R. Soc. B, 362, 2307–2331.

Chown, S.L., Lee, J.E., Hughes, K.A., Barnes, J., Barrett, P.J., Bergstrom, D.M., Convey, P., Cowan, D.A., Crosbie, K., Dyer, G., Frenot, Y., Grant, S.M., Herr, D., Kennicutt, M.C., Lamers, M., Murray, A., Possingham, H.P., Reid, K., Riddle, M.J., Ryan, P.G., Sanson, L., Shaw, J.D., Sparrow, M.D., Summerhayes, C., Terauds, A., Wall, D.H. 2012 - Challenges to the future conservation of the Antarctic. Science, 337, 158-159.

Chown, S.L., Huiskes, A.H.L., Gremmen, N.J.M., Lee, J.E, Terauds, A., Crosbie, K., Frenot, Y., Hughes, K.A., Imura, S., Kiefer, K., Lebouvier, M., Raymond, B., Tsujimotoi, M., Ware, C., Van de Vijver, B., Bergstrom, D.M. 2012 - Continent-wide risk assessment for the establishment of nonindigenous species in Antarctica. Proc. Nat. Acad. Sci. USA, 109, 4938-4943.

Chwedorzewska, K J., Korczak, M. 2010 - Human impact upon the environment in the vicinity of Arctowski Station, King George Island, Antarctica. Pol. Polar Res., 31, 45-60.

Chwedorzewska, K.J., Bednarek, P.T. 2012. - Genetic and epigenetic variation in a cosmopolitan grass Poa annua from Antarctic and Polish populations. Pol. Polar Res., 33, 63-80.

COMNAP, SCAR. 2010 - Checklists for supply chain managers of National Antarctic Programmes for the reduction in risk of transfer of non-native species. Available at: https://www.comnap.aq/Shared%20Documents/nnschecklists.pdf

Convey, P. 2011 - Antarctic terrestrial biodiversity in a changing world. Polar Biol., 34, 1629-1641.

Convey, P., Frenot, Y., Gremmen, N. & Bergstrom, D.M. 2006 - Biological Invasions. In Convey P., Huiskes A. & Bergstrom D.M. (eds) Trends in Antarctic Terrestrial and Limnetic Ecosystems. Springer, Dordrecht pp. 193-220.

Convey, P., Hughes, K. A., Tin, T. 2012 - Continental governance and environmental management mechanisms under the Antarctic Treaty System: sufficient for the biodiversity challenges of this century? Biodiversity. 13, 1–15.

Cowan, D.A., Chown, S. L., Convey, P., Tuffin, M., Hughes, K.A., Pointing, S., Vincent, W.F. 2011 - Non-indigenous microorganisms in the Antarctic - assessing the risks. Trends Microbiol., 19, 540-548.

Cuba-Díaz, M., Troncoso, J. M., Cordero, C., Finot, V.L., Rondanelli-Reyes, M. 2012 - Juncus bufonius L., a new alien vascular plant in King George Island, South Shetland Archipelago. Antarct. Sci., 25, 385–386.

Curry, C. H., McCarthy, J.S., Darragh, H.M., Wake, R.A., Todhunter, R., Terris, J. 2002. Could tourist boots act as vectors for disease transmission in Antarctica? J. Travel Med., 9, 190-193.

Dartnall, H.J.G. 2005 – Are Antarctic planktonic rotifers anthropogenic introductions? Quekett J. Microscopy, 40, 137-143.

De Poorter, M., Gilbert, N., Storey, B., Rogan-Finnemore, M. 2006 Final Report of the Workshop on "Non-native Species in the Antarctic", Christchurch, New Zealand, 10-12 April 2006.

Everatt, M.J., Worland, M.R., Bale, J.S., Convey, P., Hayward, S.A. 2012 - Pre-adapted to the maritime Antarctic? - Rapid cold hardening of the midge, Eretmoptera murphyi. J. Insect Physiol., 58, 1104-1111.

Falk-Petersen, J., Bohn, T., Sandlund, O.T. 2006. On the numerous concepts in invasion biology. Biological Invasions, 8, 1409-1424.

Frenot, Y., Chown S.L., Whinam, J., Selkirk P.M., Convey, P, Skotnicki, M., Bergstrom D.M. 2005 - Biological invasions in the Antarctic: extent, impacts and implications. Biological Rev., 80, 45-72.

Gielwanowska, I., Kellmann-Sopyla, W. 2015 – Generative reproduction of Antarctic grasses, the native species Deschampsia antarctica Desv. and the alien species Poa annua. Polish Polar Res. 36, 261-279.

Greenslade, P., Potapov, M., Russell, D., Convey, P. 2012 - Global Collembola on Deception Island. J. Insect Sci., 12, 111.

Headland, R. K. 2012 - History of exotic terrestrial mammals in Antarctic regions. Polar Rec., 48, 123-144.

Houghton, M., McQuillan, P.B., Bergstrom, D.M., Frost, L., Van Den Hoff, J., and Shaw, J. 2014 - Pathways of alien invertebrate transfer to the Antarctic region. Polar Biol., 39, 23-33.

Hughes, K.A., Convey, P. 2010 - The protection of Antarctic terrestrial ecosystems from inter- and intra-continental transfer of non-indigenous species by human activities: a review of current systems and practices. Global Environmental Change, 20, 96-112. DOI:10.1016/j. gloenvcha.2009.09.005.

Hughes, K.A., Worland, M.R. 2010 - Spatial distribution, habitat preference and colonisation status of two alien terrestrial invertebrate species in Antarctica. Antarct. Sci., 22, 221-231.

Hughes, K.A., Convey, P. 2012 - Determining the native/non-native status of newly discovered terrestrial and freshwater species in Antarctica - current knowledge, methodology and management action. J. Environ. Man., 93, 52-66.

Hughes, K.A., Convey, P. 2014 - Alien invasions in Antarctica – is anyone liable? Polar Res., 33, 22103. http://dx.doi.org/10.3402/polar.v33.22103

Hughes, K.A., Frenot, Y. 2015 - Status of known non-native species introductions and impacts. Antarctic Environments Portal Information Summary Version 1.0. https://environments.aq/information-summaries/status-of-known-non-native-species-introductions-and-impacts/

Hughes, K.A., Ashton, G.V. 2016 – Breaking the ice: the introduction of biofouling organisms to Antarctica on vessel hulls. Aquat. Conserv. DOI: 10.1002/aqc.2625.

Hughes, K.A., Walsh, S., Convey, P., Richard, S., Bergstrom, D. 2005 – Alien fly populations established at two Antarctic research stations. Polar Biol., 28, 568-570.

Hughes, K.A., Convey, P., Maslen, N.R., Smith, R.I.L. 2010 - Accidental transfer of non-native soil organisms into Antarctica on construction vehicles. Biological Invasions, 12, 875-891. DOI:10.1007/s10530-009-9508-2.

Hughes, K.A., Lee, J.E., Ware, C., Kiefer, K., Bergstrom, D.M. 2010 - Impact of anthropogenic transportation to Antarctica on alien seed viability. Polar Biol., 33, 1123-1130.

Hughes, K.A., Lee, J.E., Tsujimoto, M., Imura, S., Bergstrom, D.M., Ware, C., Lebouvier, M., Huiskes, A.H.L., Gremmen, N.J.M., Frenot, Y., Bridge, P.D., Chown, S. L. 2011 - Food for thought: risks of non-native species transfer to the Antarctic region with fresh produce. Biological Conservation, 144, 1682–1689.

Hughes, K.A., Fretwell, P., Rae, J. Holmes, K., Fleming, A. 2011 - Untouched Antarctica: mapping a finite and diminishing environmental resource. Antarct. Sci., 23, 537-548.

Hughes, K.A., Worland, M.R., Thorne, M., Convey, P. 2013 - The non-native chironomid Eretmoptera murphyi in Antarctica: erosion of the barriers to invasion. Biological Invasions, 15, 269-281.

Hughes, K.A., Huiskes, A.H.L, Convey, P. 2014 - Global movement and homogenisation of biota: challenges to the environmental management of Antarctica? In T. Tin, D. Liggett, P. Maher, and M. Lamers (eds). The Future of Antarctica: Human impacts, strategic planning and values for conservation. Springer, Dordrecht. DOI: 10.1007/978-94-007-6582-5_5

Hughes, K.A., Cowan, D.A., and Wilmotte, A. 2015 - Protection of Antarctic microbial communities – 'Out of sight, out of mind'. Front. Microbiol. DOI: 10.3389/fmicb.2015.00151

Hughes, K.A., Pertierra, L.R., Molina-Montenegro, M., Convey, P. 2015. Biological invasions in Antarctica: what it the current status and can we respond? Biodivers. Conserv., 24, 1031-1055.

Huiskes, A.H.L., Gremmen, N.J.M., Bergstrom, D.M., Frenot, Y., Hughes, K.A., Imura, S., Kiefer, K., Lebouvier, M., Lee, J.E., Tsujimoto, M., Ware, C., Van de Vijver, B., Chown, S.L. 2014 - Aliens in Antarctica: Assessing transfer of plant propagules by human visitors to reduce invasion risk. Biol. Conserv., 171, 278-284.

Kerry, K.R., Riddle, M. (Eds.) 2009 - Health of Antarctic Wildlife: A Challenge for Science and Policy, Springer Verlag, ISBN-13: 9783540939221.

Lee, J.E., Chown, S.L. 2009 – Mytilus on the move: transport of an invasive bivalve to the Antarctic. Mar. Ecol. Prog. Ser., 339, 307-310.

Lee, J.E., Chown, S.L. 2009 – Breaching the dispersal barrier to invasion: quantification and management. Ecol. Appl., 19, 1944-1959.

Lee, J.E., Chown, S.L. 2009 – Temporal development of hull-fouling assemblages associated with an Antarctic supply vessel. Mar. Ecol. Prog. Ser., 396, 97-105.

Lee, J.E., Chown, S.L. 2011 - Quantification of intra-regional propagule movements in the Antarctic. Antarct. Sci., 23, 337-342.

Lewis, P.N., Bergstrom, D.M., Whinam, J. 2006 – Barging in: A temperate marine community travels to the subantarctic. Biol. Invasions, 8, 787-795.

Lewis, P.N., Hewitt, C.L., Riddle, M., McMinn, A. 2003. Marine introductions in the Southern Ocean: an unrecognised hazard to biodiversity. Mar. Pollut. Bull., 46, 213-223.

Litynska-Zajac, M., Chwedorzewska, K., Olech, M., Korczak-Abshire, M., Augustyniuk-Kram, A. 2012 - Diaspores and phyto-remains accidentally transported to the Antarctic Station during three expeditions. Biodivers. Conserv., 21, 3411-3421.

McGeoch, M.A., Shaw, J.D., Terauds, A., Lee, J.E., Chown, S.L. 2015 - Monitoring biological invasion across the broader Antarctic: A baseline and indicator framework. Glob. Environ. Change. DOI: 10.1016/j.gloenvcha.2014.12.012

Molina-Montenegro, M., Carrasco-Urra, F., Rodrigo, C., Convey, P., Valladares, F., Gianoli, E. 2012 - Occurrence of the non-native annual bluegrass (Poa annua) on the Antarctic mainland and its negative effects on native plants. Conserv. Biol., 26, 717-723.

Molina-Montenegro, M., Carrasco-Urra, F., Acuna-Rodriquez, I., Oses, R., Torres-Díaz, C., Chwedorzewska, K.J. 2014 - Assessing the importance of human activities for the establishment of the invasive Poa annua in Antarctica. Polar Res., 33, 21425. http://dx.doi.org/10.3402/polar.v33.21425

Molina-Montenegro, M.A., Pertierra, L.R., Razeto-Barry, P., Díaz, J., Finot, V.L., Torres-Díaz, C. 2015 - A recolonization record of the invasive Poa annua in Paradise Bay, Antarctic Peninsula: modeling of the potential spreading risk. Polar Biol., 38, 1091-1096. DOI: 10.1007/s00300-015-1668-1

Newman, J., Coetzee, B.W.T., Chown, S.L., Terauds, A., McIvor, E. 2014 - The introduction of non-native species to the Antarctic. Antarctic Environments Portal Information Summary Version 1.0. http://environments.aq/information-summaries/the-introduction-of-non-native-species-to-antarctica/

Nielsen, U.N., Wall, D.H. 2013 - The future of soil invertebrate communities in polar regions: different climate change responses in the Arctic and Antarctic? Ecol. Lett., 16, 409-419.

Olech, M., Chwedorzewska, K.J. 2011 - The first appearance and establishment of an alien vascular plant in natural habitats on the forefield of a retreating glacier in Antarctica. Antarct. Sci., 23, 153-154.

Osyczka, P. 2010 - Alien lichens unintentionally transported to the "Arctowski" station (South Shetlands, Antarctica). Polar Biol., 33, 1067-1073.

Osyczka, P., Mleczko, P., Karasinski, D., Chlebicki, A. 2012 - Timber transported to Antarctica: a potential and undesirable carrier for alien fungi and insects. Biol. Invasions, 14, 15-20.

Pearce, D.A., Hughes, K.A., Lachlan-Cope, T., Harangozo, S.A., Jones, A.E. 2010 - Biodiversity of air-borne microorganisms at Halley station, Antarctica. Extremophiles, 14, 145-159.

Pertierra, L.R., Lara, F., Benayas, J., Hughes, K.A. 2013. Poa pratensis L., current status of the longest-established non-native vascular plant in the Antarctic. Polar Biol., 36, 1473-1481.

Potter, S. 2006 - The Quarantine Management of Australia's Antarctic Program. Australasian. J. Environ. Man., 13, 185-195.

Potter, S. 2009 - Protecting Antarctica from Non-Native Species: The Imperatives and the Impediments. In G. Alfredsson and T. Koivurova (eds), D. Leary sp. ed. The Yearbook of Polar Law, vol. 1, pp. 383-400.

Ranjith, L., Shukla, S.P., Vennila, A., Gashaw, T.D. 2012 - Bioinvasion in Antarctic Ecosystems. Proc. Nat. Acad. Sci. India Sect. B – Biol. Sci., 82, 353-359.

Reisinger, R. R., McIntyre, T., Bester, M. N. 2010 - Goose barnacles hitchhike on satellite-tracked southern elephant seals. Polar Biol., 33, 561-564.

Russell, D.J., Hohberg, K., Otte, V., Christian, A., Potapov, M., Brückner, A., McInnes, S.J. 2013 - The impact of human activities on soil organisms of the maritime Antarctic and the introduction of non-native species in Antarctica.

Federal Environment Agency (Umweltbundesamt). http://www.uba.de/uba-info-medien-e/4416.html

Russell, D. J., Hohberg, K., Potapov, M., Brückner, A., Otte, V., Christian, A. 2014 - Native terrestrial invertebrate fauna from the northern Antarctic Peninsula: new records, state of current knowledge and ecological preferences – Summary of a German federal study. Soil Org., 86, 1-58.

SATCM XII - WP 6 (Australia) 2000 - Diseases of Antarctic Wildlife.

Smith, R.I.L. 1996 - Introduced plants in Antarctica: potential impacts and conservations issues. Biol. Conserv., 76, 135–146.

Smith, R.I.L., Richardson, M. 2011 - Fuegian plants in Antarctica: natural or anthropogenically assisted immigrants? Biol. Invasions, 13, 1-5.

Tavares, M., De Melo, G.A.S. 2004 – Discovery of the first known benthic invasive species in the Southern Ocean: the North Atlantic spider crab Hyas araneus found in the Antarctic Peninsula. Antarct. Sci., 16, 129-131.

Terauds, A., Chown, S.L., Morgan, F., Peat, H.J., Watts, D.J., Keys, H., Convey, P., Bergstrom, D.M. 2012 - Conservation biogeography of the Antarctic. Divers. Distrib., 18, 726-741.

Tin, T., Fleming, Z.L., Hughes, K.A., Ainley, D.G., Convey, P., Moreno, C.A., Pfeiffer, S., Scott, J., Snape, I. 2009 - Impacts of local human activities on the Antarctic environment. Antarct. Sci., 21, 3-33.

Tsujimoto, M., Imura, S. 2012 - Does a new transportation system increase the risk of importing non-native species to Antarctica? Antarct. Sci., 24, 441-449.

Tsujimoto, M., Imura, S. 2013 - Biosecurity measures being implemented at Australian Antarctic Division against non-native species introduction into Antarctica. Antarct. Rec., 57, 137-150.

Walther, G.-R., Roques, A., Hulme, P.E., Sykes, M.T., Pysek, P., Kühn, I., Zobel, M. 2009. Alien species in a warmer world: risks and opportunities. Trends Ecol. Evol., 24, 686-693. DOI:10.1016/j.tree.2009.06.008.

Whinam, J., Chilcott, N., Bergstrom, D.M. 2005 – Subantarctic hitchhikers: expeditioners as vectors for the introduction of alien organisms. Biol. Conserv., 21, 207-219.

Whinam, J. 2009 - Aliens in the Sub-Antarctic - Biosecurity and climate change. Papers and Proceedings of the Royal Society of Tasmania, 143, 45-52.

Wódkiewicz, M., Galera, H., Chwedorzewska, K.J., Gielwanowska, I., Olech, M. 2013 - Diaspores of the introduced species Poa annua L. in soil samples from King George Island (South Shetlands, Antarctica). Arct. Antarct. Alp. Res. 45: 415-419.

Wodkiewicz, M, Ziemianski, M., Kwiecien, K., Chwedorzewska, K.J., Galera, H. 2014 - Spatial structure of the soil seed bank of Poa annua L.- alien species in the Antarctic. Biodivers. Conserv., 23, 1339-1346.

Volonterio, O., de León, R.P., Convey, P., Krzeminska, E. 2013 - First record of Trichoceridae (Diptera) in the maritime Antarctic. Polar Biol., 36, 1125-1131.

Secretariat of the Antarctic Treaty

Maipú 757 Piso 4 (C1006ACI) – Buenos Aires – Argentina

www.ats.aq

ats@ats.aq

www.ingramcontent.com/pod-product-compliance
Lightning Source LLC
Chambersburg PA
CBHW081652270326
41933CB00018B/3441